Sharing

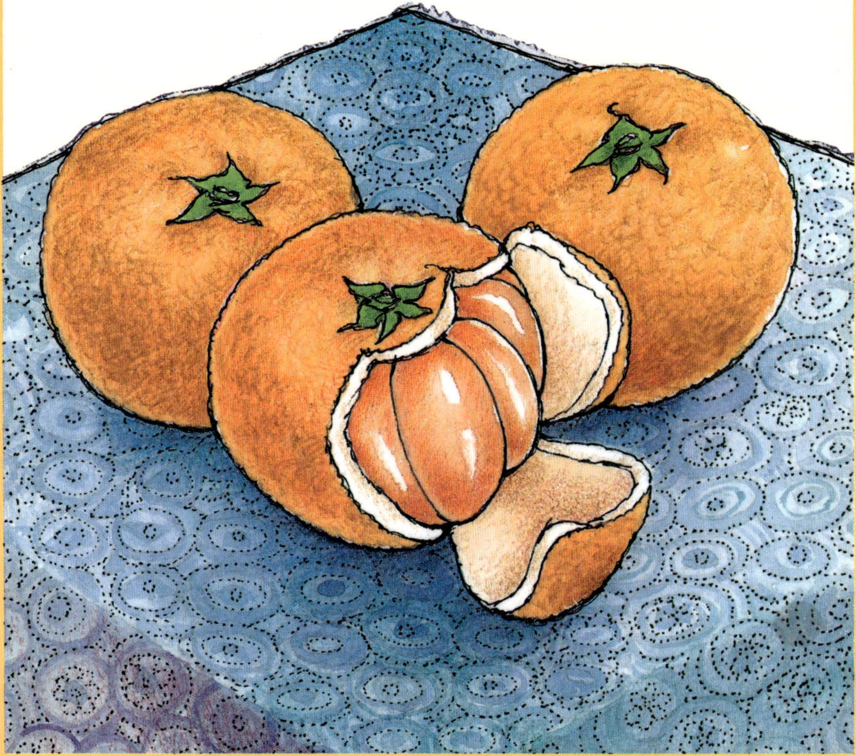

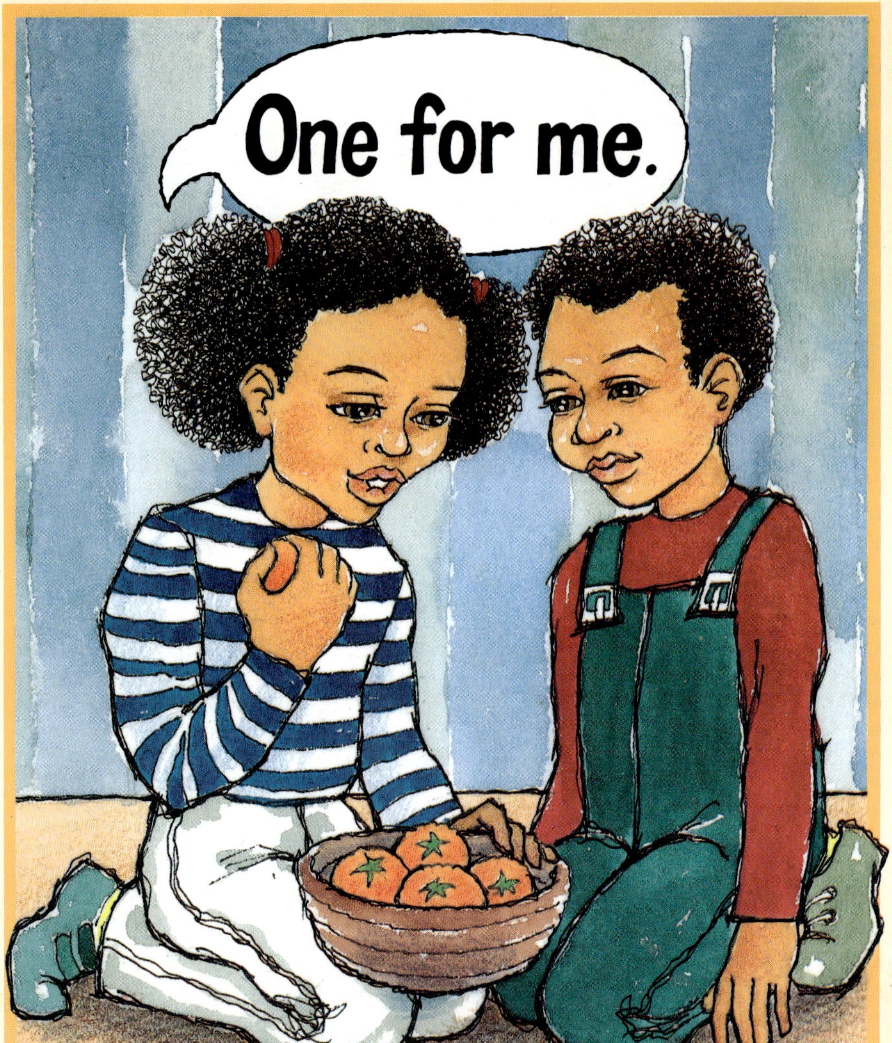
One for me.

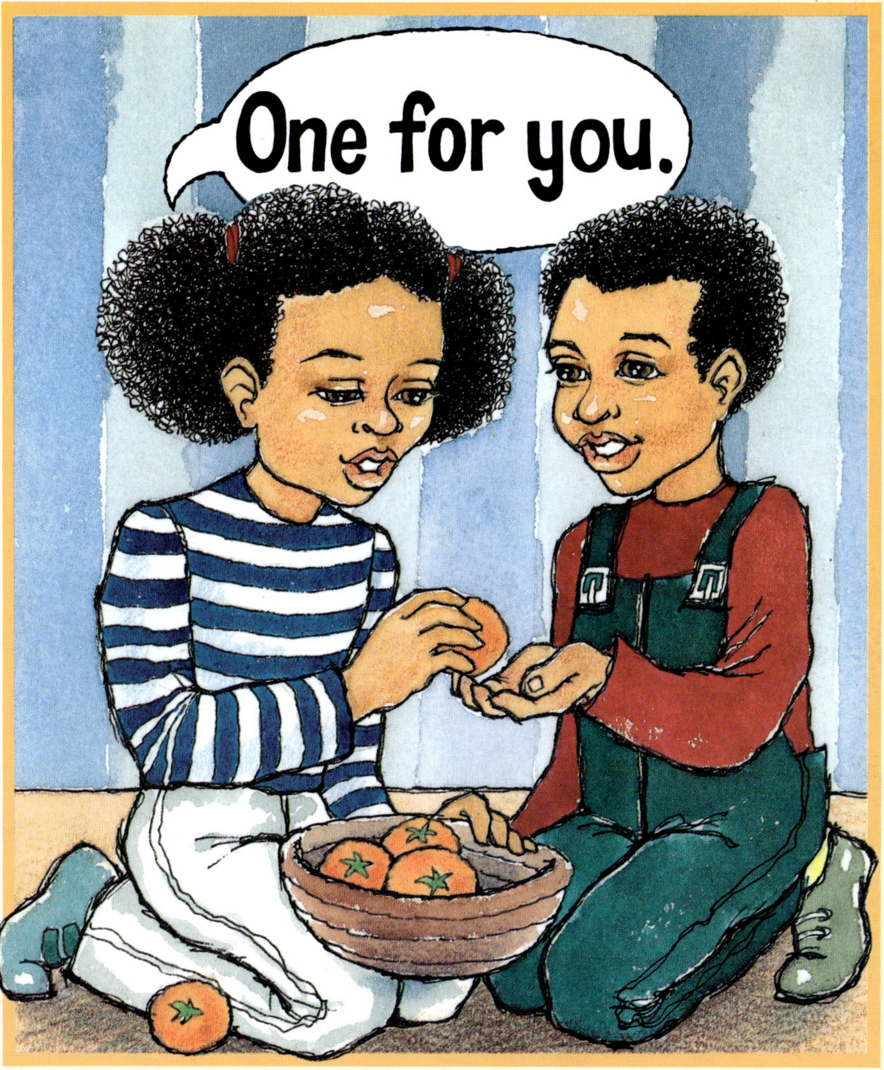
One for you.

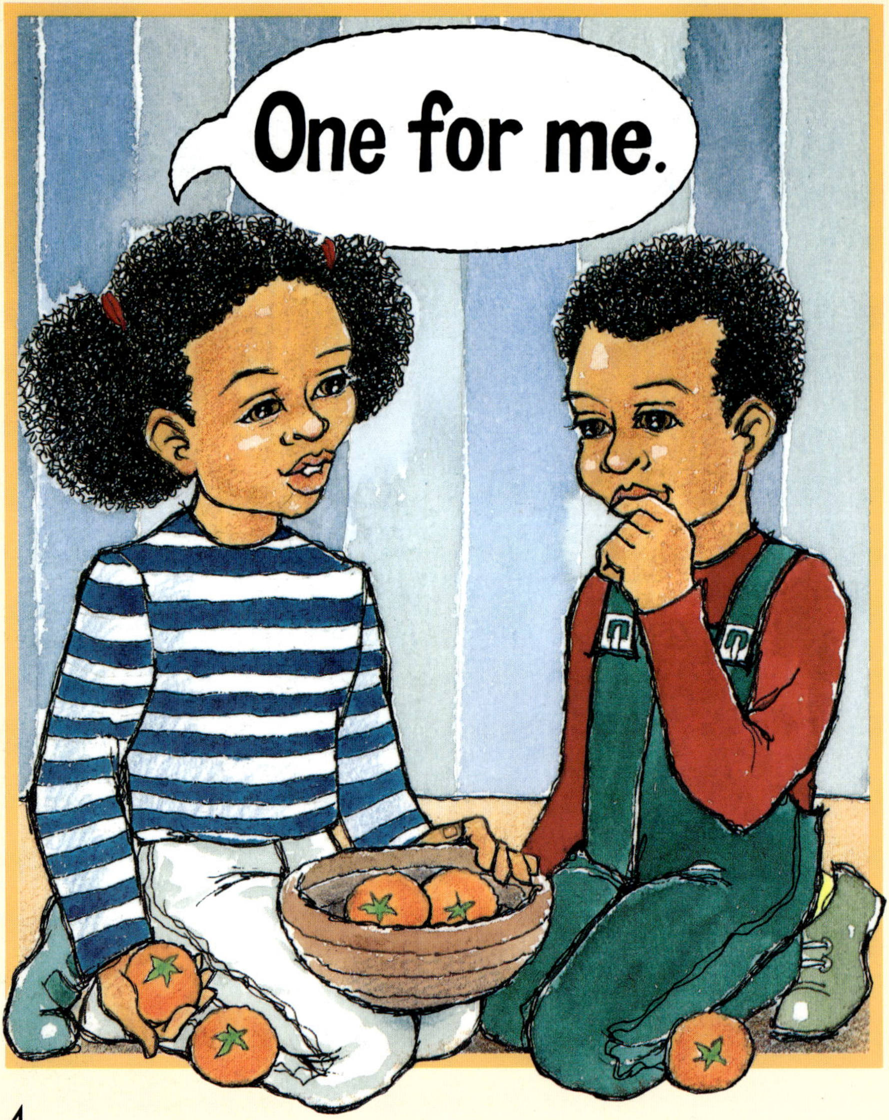
One for me.

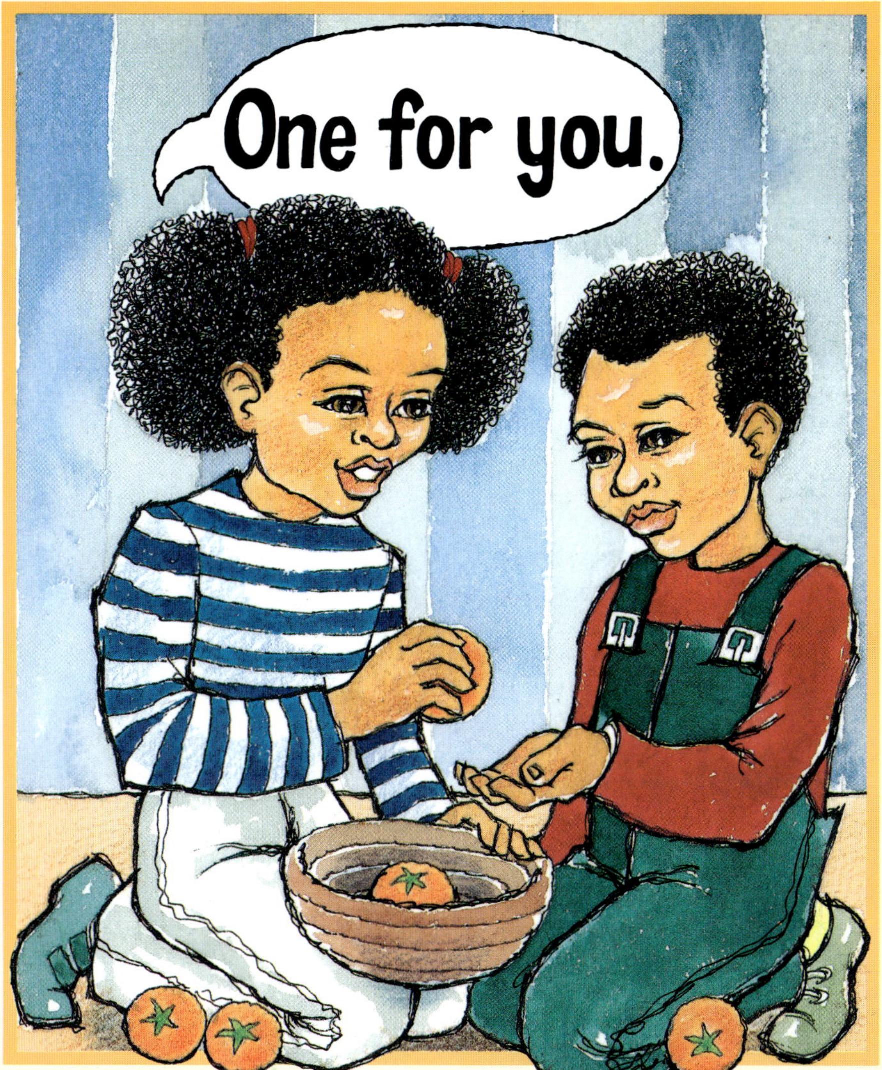
One for you.

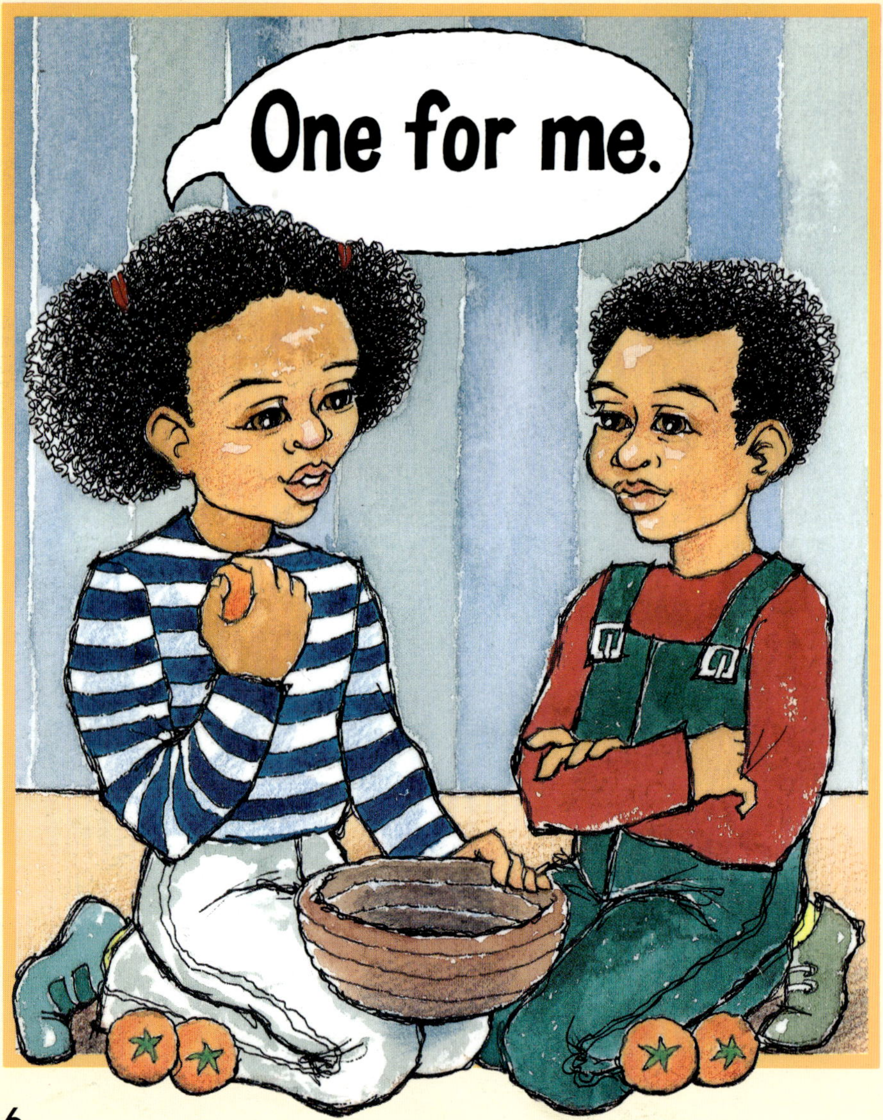
One for me.

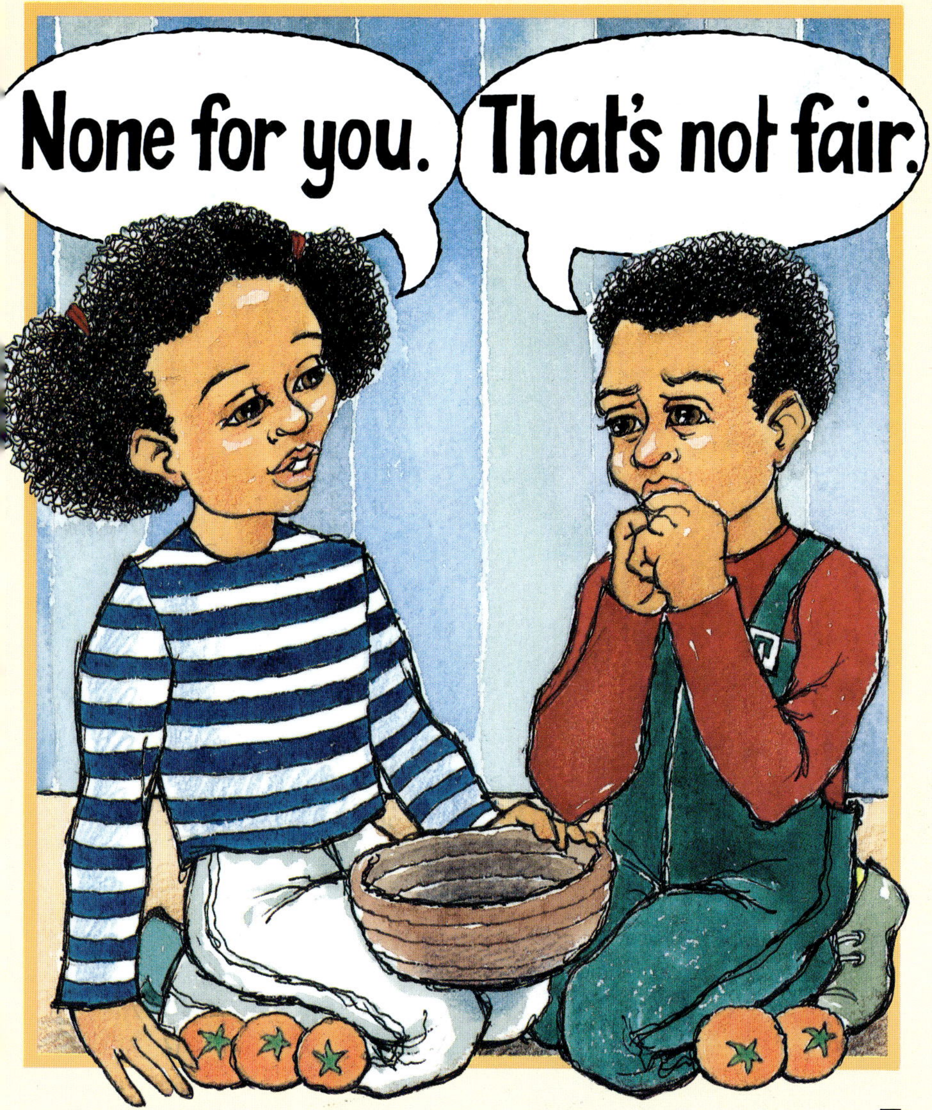
None for you.
That's not fair.

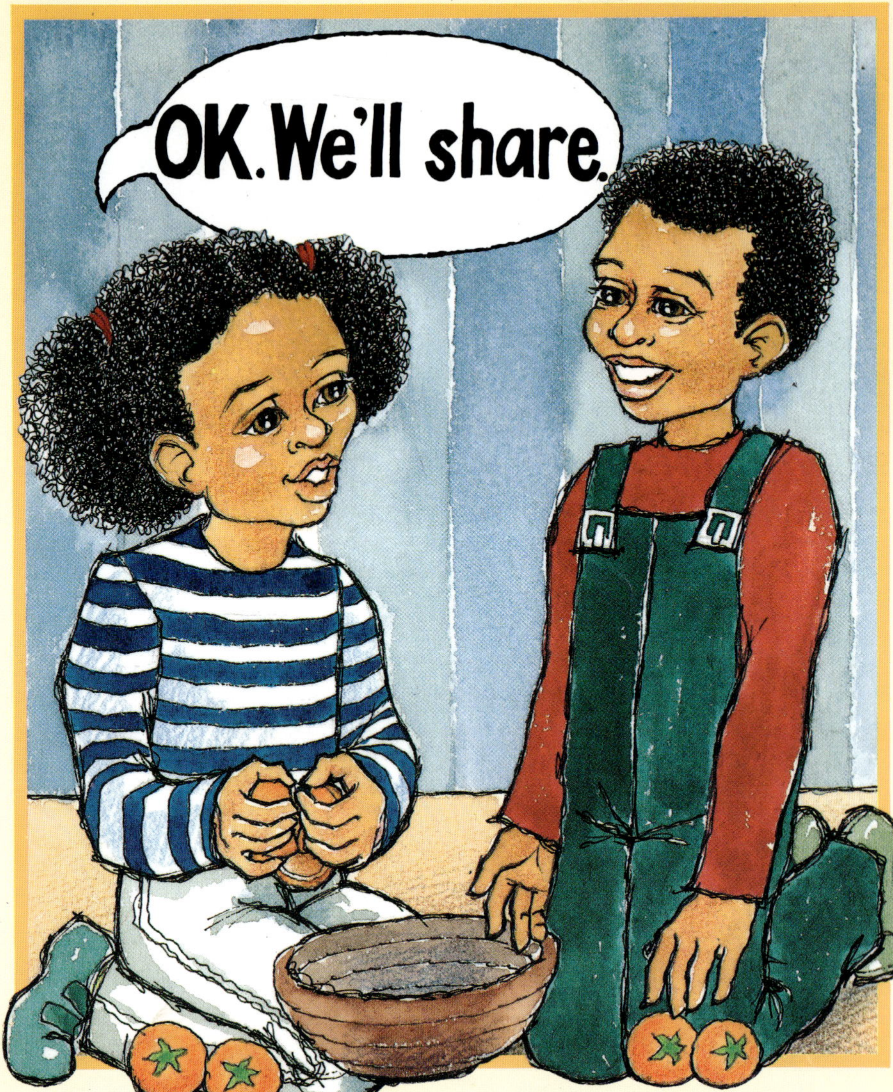
OK. We'll share.